DUST DEVILS
COZY CORNERS
and JAVELINAS

A Newcomer's Tale of Tucson

MICHELEE MORGAN CABOT

Dust Devils, Cozy Corners, and Javelinas:
A Newcomer's Tale of Tucson

Published by Wheatmark®
2030 East Speedway Boulevard, Suite 106
Tucson, Arizona 85719 USA
www.wheatmark.com

ISBN: 978-1-62787-652-0 (paperback)
ISBN: 978-1-62787-653-7 (ebook)
LCCN: 2018956603

rev201901

CONTENTS

CONTENTS

"You know, we don't *have* to stay here."

He stood there, breathing hard from snow shoveling, ear flaps brushing his raised collar in protection against the near-zero temperature. A telltale patch of frostbite was starting on his cheek.

"Our parents are gone; the kids are on their own. And I'm retired. Enough of this. We could move south." He looked at me eagerly, hopefully.

A crystalline dawn danced on leafless ice-coated trees, flashing tiny rainbow prisms. It was a wonderland of glistening ice. A branch cracked and snapped from its weight.

A front had passed through the night, clearing chilling fogs and leaving behind a breathtaking snowfall. My recently retired husband had been working at removing a new drift from in front of the door. It was face-nipping cold out there atop our New England hill in our hometown for thirty-five years.

He is my companion of heart and sky, my fellow traveler for life, including piloting our plane to the aqua waters of the Bahamas and happy mariachi of Mexico, as well as across our own nation. I looked back at him. I thought, *I'm shivering in a house whose central heat is struggling to keep us warm. Real estate taxes are out of sight. Oil costs have soared this winter. We use the fireplace a lot.*

My ear caught the sounds of trickling water calling from the front of the house, and I knew that a roof-edge ice dam was again wreaking damage to the sun room.

Move south? Sounded good to me.

"Really? You mean it? Oh, honey, could I ever do that!" My Texas born-and-raised self quivered. "But where would we go?"

"Your family is in San Antonio—we could start there," he said.

And so it was that we began thinking of an escape plan.

It was going around. A few friends had long since opted for Florida winters; we considered that. Intriguingly close to the Bahamas and Exumas, it had a strong allure. But when a couple of retirees to Arizona joyfully exclaimed, "Michelee, we have found your place! A colonial town in Mexico!" we thought about it.

And went.

The upshot was that we found enormous charm and color South of the Border, in a place that filled my need for constant sunshine and flowers. And maybe best of all, a bountiful supply of help, both for house and garden. And it had a lovely culture.

We launched into it, built a home of arches and vistas, and made expat friends. We also adjusted to being in a place not anywhere near our tribe and settled in to making this erstwhile Spanish-colonial silver-mining town, Álamos, our hub for travel. Being a licensed pilot, I had begun flying years before and had lured my mate into it. Aerial exploring and travel adventuring had been our life for many years, and we wanted to keep it up.

Álamos had an airport and a group of pilots hangered there. It seemed perfect. And so it was.

The Mexican morning dawned clear and bright, promising the kind of day we had become used to in our sunny paradise. A favorite mixing bowl snatched for dog food was already rocking gently from a crow perching insolently on its rim. Its beady gold-ringed eye caught mine. I could swear he shrugged.

Hilarious how sassy blackbirds love doggie croquets. All backyard flyers, really. They tickle me, and I suffer the muttering from my dear heart husband as he fusses about the cost.

"They're eating the dog food," he grouches. "What's wrong with their birdseed?" A cardinal's red crest moves in the bougainvillea. It fidgets and glares down at the crow.

Beautiful, bucolic, blissful. We stared across the table at each other.

Uh oh... we were feeling a little bored. Bored? How could that be? Our days were full of grownup play-dates— (no children among our group, mostly retirees)—luncheon gatherings for Rummy Tiles, bridge, poker, a fun new domino game of Mexican Train, and so on. Evenings we clustered at the watering holes for sippings and snackings, enjoying each other's company. Alamos attracted an interesting group of ex-pats, from artists to scientists to writers. One writer had a cadre who put on her clever plays depicting life in town. Sadly that effort died with her—it was an era gone. That no longer a diversion, we looked beyond the town. Ah, the pull of the countryside! Delightedly we sortied and explored throughout the area, gathering goods to feather our nest—cantera items in Los Mochis, carved leather art in Mazatlan, indigenous masks from the local Indians. Trips to the beach were always a good take. We liked the mariscos (fish) restaurants at the shore, where freshness put the kibosh on store bought.

The Nortemericano community in Alamos was well established, mostly snowbirds from Canada and certain of our northern states. We newbies chatted them up. We ourselves had foregone all real estate ties to the USA, in the cause of tax savings. But these Alamensens were mostly only half-year residents, needing to fulfill certain legal residential requirements. Their escape routes to needed variety were in place. They discussed our ennui among themselves, and shared a point of view. "Get a place up north to scamper to, have your kids visit."

We had a discussion. OK then. Maybe we should poke

around handy Tucson, and get one ourselves. We reviewed the options, discussed it with the help. All was good.

Our muchachas promised they would watch after the place, take care of the dogs, and feed those busy little birds.

We loaded our little Cessna, said our adios to the crew, and flew off to see what we would see. We looked, bought, and started nesting. Again. We already knew Tucson to be a fun place, and Medicare was extant. So why not?

Our adventures continue, and I am compelled to tell you about it.

Grab hold—Tucson, here we come!

1 FLYING IN

Do I Fly Over, Under, or Around . . .

That morning had dawned "severe clear," right up to Flight Level God. (Av speak is so colorful.)

Our usual airport departure routine: underwing prayers with the charismatic preacher / airport manager, climb in, belt up, go through the checklist (yep, chocks removed from wheels—a red-faced moment when you forget them, while gunning the engine and the plane fruitlessly humpety-bumps on the chocks, rail-birds laughing on the sidelines). Out to the runway, give takeoff rpms, scoot quickly, and lift off.

We had splendid weather as we waved adios to our helper *hombres* from Álamos. A half hour later, we touched down at Cuidad Obregón to document departing the country with tiresome government paperwork.

With the idea of a house search in Tucson, a little something for when we needed to go to "the other side" on US business, we happily began winging our blue-sky flight from Mexico and our sun-seeking northern snowbirds. Hotels can be mighty nice, but not as sweet as your own digs.

An hour after that, we had covered two-thirds of the route, passing the point of no return.

Oh dear. Ahead, it wasn't all that open any more. We had foolishly drawn out the departure. A forecasted weather change was happening sooner than expected. Clouds were fluffing and stacking, a threatening monsoon skyscape, a line promising to fill in and dump interesting weather on us. We knew the air would get rough as rising air formed more clouds, crackling lightning as they purpled up.

As forecasted, ominous piles of cumulonimbus were popping up ahead, signs of storms on a grand scale. So far, they seemed innocuous, but we definitely had to get beyond them. Still nothing on the "fright finder," the sensor on the panel that registers data on electrical storms up to two hundred miles ahead. This was the Mexican monsoon season, and we knew it was only a matter of time before they soared high to burst ripping energy.

I figured to stay the course, deviating just a bit here and there to dodge between build-ups. My navigator husband and favorite cockpit mate said, "Ah, um, why not go below the ceiling? You'll be able to see the mountains—the highest is only fifty-five hundred feet in this sector." He was looking at the chart.

Maybe sí, maybe no. There could be unpleasant instability under there. But his nagging kept coming to "just go below." That played with my head.

I put on the speed brakes, added flaps, took off some power, and started down. Then I waffled, thinking better of it. *On* with the power and *off* with the air brakes, leveling out. "Let's just stay at this altitude," I muttered. But the clouds were assembling impressively, getting higher and thicker. Nuts.

Into the descent again. Nose down, power back, flaps to angle the forward downward view better—and on top of the wings the speed brakes again went up, spoiling a bit of lift and slowing us down.

"You're being a danged yo-yo," I scolded myself. Stupid.

We floated down, and down, and down, but hey, still not below the ceiling.

This was not working out.

Peering through the windscreen, I saw blue-black shadows spreading over sharp lumpy ridges—and dense rain swelling from slate-bottomed cloud bases. Thick, mean curtains of rain. No going under there. So much for suggestions. But sometimes you don't know till you take a look.

A course change was required, right now.

Looking west, I could see a clean run up the valley to Nogales, the city just south of Tucson. Cranking ninety degrees left, off we shot westward a few miles. Once we'd safely bypassed that stew of energy, a brisk right turn put us back on our northerly course.

But we weren't out of it yet. Forward visibility was excellent, but to the left a jagged bolt ripped cloud to ground. Off the right wing drifted the deep misty blue of heavy rain. The buildup we had just circumnavigated had grown fast. Storm clouds can blossom upward by thousands of feet per minute, as had this one. There were splendid storms erupting all around us.

By now the radio was crackling out Tucson approach's advisory of bad weather. We said oh we knew, cells were in plain sight and, so far, easy to duck. From where we were, we could practically see Tucson International's runways through paths between the cells. "But, Approach, the cloud cover is filling in."

"A pilot, report please. What are your observations, zero-five-alpha?"

"We're finding the cloud base at eight thousand feet, but rapidly lowering," I replied and added that where there was precip and zero visibility. He cleared me down to four thousand direct to the airport. Soon we were taxiing to customs—and scampering into the office before the rain came.

It was a drenching that didn't come. That one stayed in the foothills. A week later, Tucson's yearly monsoon finally began, fraught with microbursts and foothill floods. Those are days when you're glad to be on the ground inside something strong.

With your wings hangered.

And so we experienced our first flying entry into Tucson from South of the Border. We didn't know it yet, but this friendly city would be the place for a house to perch in when we wanted to "get off the island," the expat's whimsical reference to our colonial Pueblo Mágico, Álamos.

As much as we love our Mexican home, we are surely norteamericanos, accustomed to its certain senses, sensibilities—and conveniences.

2 DESERT TOWN, GLOBAL CULTURE

As children, many of us were unknowingly baptized into the classics. Who didn't sit spellbound by tales of *The Lone Ranger* and its William Tell Overture (bada-boom! bada-boom! bada-boom-boom-boom!) tattooing our brains? Or Wagner's Ring Cycle, condensed into Elmer Fudd's hilarious, sword-brandishing fifteen-minute "Kill the wabbit! Kill the wabbit!"? Some, less patient than others and not so smitten by the full three-day opus, mutter that the Ring has never been done better.

Tucson, the cosmopolitan city on the desert. Desert, yes. Culturally deprived, no. Sensory delights were there to be wallowed in. The resort spas, the savory cuisines, the stunning horizons of towering mountains, the bright-eyed wildlife—all have their unique attraction. Including music. The Tucson Symphony Orchestra, particularly. The culture is alive with creative jazz, good trios, excellent vocal groups—but the symphony is the pride of the city. Extant since 1928, the TSO draws all, from youth to seniors, into the spectacularly sensuous world of magnificent opuses, old and new.

Tucson Music Hall's acoustics are as good as the best in the world. The talents it showcases are the best in the world. Violinist Midori, cellist Yo-Yo Ma, the Trans- Siberian Orchestra, right there at your feet. And opera? Nearby Phoenix's opera brings in two performances a year, which are quick sell-outs. During our first Tucson adventuring prowl, we headed for the hall to take in Handel's *Julius Caesar*, unusual in that a principal's role was to be sung by a coloratura soprano, a part usually cast with a male voice.

But what ho? What was that powerful operatic voice filtering through our motel room door? The afternoon of the concert, lyrical and familiar notes arose from the room across our hallway, filling our heads with snippets of melody and arpeggios. An opera performer, clearly a star, was warming up. Would she be in our opera that night?

She was, and what a hit. The next day, upon again hearing trilling, rippling melismas, I knocked on her door.

A handsome young woman, with big eyes and masses of dark wavy hair, peered out.

"Hello, beautiful voice!" said I, smiling at her. "Please, I hope we're not interrupting?" I explained we were just across the hall and heard her vocalizing through the walls. "We heard you singing yesterday afternoon, and prayed we'd hear you last night—and we did! Your singing was fabulous, inspirational."

She beamed at the compliment. "Taking a male role was risky. And I had to hide all this hair," she said, running fingers through it.

"Well, you pulled it off brilliantly! See the review?" I waved the newspaper at her. "The critics say so, too!"

So Tucson's venue spectacularly delivers.

But a heads-up. The span from designated parking to the hall's lofty entrance is extensive. It poses a looooong trek across acres of concrete. For daily walkers, not a problem. For the less spritely, get there early and put your vehicle around the back of the building where hall access is close and easy.

We have not mastered it. For us, it's always a frantic, puffing arrival just at start time. One can idiotically end up an exhausting hike-and-a-half away. Those loathsome degenerating lumbar disks shriek, you hunch over like an apostrophe on legs, you lurch fast and frantically to make the warning bell. You wheeze to your seat during the orchestra's cacophonic warm-up, barely having time to plop down and get in the mood. But with a bottom wiggle and a sigh, you do.

Just get there early, you hear? Better yet, take a cab.

Ah, Tucson, home of the UA, place of fine higher learning. If studies are your shtick, the university's abundance of free lectures are waiting. Evening schedules list a cornucopia of subjects. This university town loves to share knowledge. Besides night school as it were, there's a full slate of university-sponsored brown bag lunch lectures on subjects ranging from area water issues and community food studies, to politics and policy.

And of course, there's art—galleries abound, talent abounds. Sniffing for deals, we have cruised special exhibitions and not gone home empty-handed. Wildly colorful and painterly abstracts? Stunning collections to choose from. Representative styles more your taste? Portraits, landscapes, shimmering flights of birds…they're there. And oh dear, once you've found a piece to cherish, you need it framed. Not a problem. A city bursting with so much art and culture has many skilled artisans to help you out. You can Yelp them and see the reviews. You'll just have to get something.

For audiences who need to see thespians treading the boards, Tucson has plenty to offer. When Broadway shows come to town go to UA Centennial Hall, and for family fun head to the Gaslight Theater.

Tucson life is sweet, Tucson life is colorful, Tucson life is good.

Welcome home.

3 THE PACK RATS

A.k.a. Wood Rat

Mr. Pack Rat likes soap

Our city search paid off. Among the popular good-weather draws of the West—traffic-choked LA, high-altitude Santa Fe, San Diego of super beaches—we found that colorful Tucson promised to be easiest to settle into. We would enjoy its fun and fruits, and be ready to junket back to Old Mexico, back to the home base of our hearts. Our quest could have been daunting, but we took our time. And since this city is an amazing, welcoming town, we regularly rolled happily through show homes, restaurants, and distinctive neighborhood clusters, checking it all out, till the decision was clear and easy.

House-hunting in the desert was a new experience, browsing over the rocky, cactus-studded hills and dales of Tucson. We'd acclimated ourselves to the hot Sonoran Desert with some good living in Sonora, Mexico, so we quite liked what we saw. The warmth suited our clothes.

Peering down at bluish chunks in the graveled driveway, I blurted out to the real estate agent, "That's soap! Why is Irish Spring soap trash out here?"

"Oh, that wards off pack rats," she replied. "They can be annoying—everyone has them out here, but they can be controlled. They're repelled by Irish Spring." Later we learned otherwise, when a neighbor snorted and told us how the rodents love to line their burrows with it.

So it didn't work for her, but many do rely on it and swear by it. You can try it.

Seeking to distract us, the real estate agent gestured to some admirable cactus groupings, popular xeriscaping. Not much water out here, and one makes do with Mother Nature. To maximize the attractiveness of your desert property, best to use what the desert offers. The owners here had done a splendid job.

"The dramatic saguaro cactus, whose bloom is the Arizona state blossom, is our icon," she said. "See how many this property has?"

We were besotted with the property—a wonderful view of the city spread out in the distance—and intended to make an offer. We would deal with the pack rats.

Images from childhood flickered through my mind. I again heard my father bellowing as he found acorn bits on his dresser *right there* where his money clip had been. As their name implies, the critters steal and swap. One imagines a little wee conscience plying payments for thievery. I envisioned vermin scurrying with bright shiny things in their paws and teeth, stuff they've stolen and are hauling back to their nests—keys, buttons, bits of foil from gum packets, a diamond ring? Like magpies, any shiny thing that hits their fancy is fair game, and they leave behind, perhaps, a discarded nut as payment. Strange varmint. In my childhood home, rustlings in the walls and on rooftops turned out to be, yes, pack rats.

I didn't fancy having any on my beat. And I knew they were already there, as witness the messy display in the driveway gravel. I was undaunted. The location was primo. I would deal with them.

We bought the house, then called in Mr. Pack Rat,

the ecologically kind capturer and releaser of the furtive beasties. He educated us: "Prevention is kinder, cheaper, and more effective than extermination."

He pointed out bits of trash collected in one little area around a prickly pear. "That's a sign to look for," he said. "They make their homes in cactus root systems, creating walls of thorny spines for protection. Pretty smart, these guys." We nodded, glassy-eyed. "And you must clean up piles of brush debris around your acreage. They love those for nesting."

He rid us of all the nests he could find, and going forward, we did what he recommended. The previous owners had been a combo couple of artist and professor, minds adrift on concerns other than pack rats, thereby establishing the perfect tranquil environment for ratty living.

Our neighborhood is a well-established wildlife area. Snakes wriggle out to raise their cold body temps in the sunshine, right there on your brick path. Hawks circle and peer down to target your koi. Quail arrange eggs under blossoming bushes. Doves nest in outside wall lights. And pack rats scurry about under prickly pears, thorn-fortified homes their bases for foraging.

The brazen little beasts particularly like tasty car engine wires. No garage? Hang a work light under the hood as a "Keep off" sign. Funny how rodents worldwide like engine compartments. Back in the day, our aging Martha's Vineyard airport car grew pee-stinky over the winter from rats' nests, to the point where we simply gave it away to a mechanic. Today? Here in Tucson, we gave up the fight and made a rat–proof garage out of the come-hither carport.

What to do? Prevention is no doubt best.

And if you don't have a garage, save wear and tear on your nerves by putting one in. There are even some good prefabs.

And there's always the light under the hood.

4 PATIO GUESTS

A Precis and Hint of What's to Come

Cooper's hawk checks for prey

Our patio fountain, home to a few flitty goldfish (not koi, no chin whiskers) is a big draw for the Cooper's hawk. This fly-in hunter regards it as his private buffet. The fish, on the other hand, do not—and are uncooperative. They flee into their shadowy hideouts under lily pads and tumbled pots; they must detect his approach from way off. Coop soars in and lands on the top of the fountain. From this perch, he scowls intently down at the water, hoping, hoping. In vain. Frustrated, he settles his bottom half in the second tier of the fountain, and dips himself repeatedly, bobbing up and down in the water, fluffing and flapping his tail feathers in a whimsical cooling cleansing. It's his spa.

When he's done, he flies aloft and dries himself on the roof, whence he sorties over to the neighbors' to check for edibles. He's handsome; I'm glad he considers us worthy. But the finches and the goldfish are relieved to see him go. At his approach, the smaller birds had flown away in a frenzied startle, fanning out to make poor targets. Now they return to the thistle and sunflower seeds; doves, too, resume their ground-level pickings from the feeder debris. And all take their own turns at the fountain. Late afternoon comes; the desert sun's rays angle in to light up red and yellow finch breasts as they take their last sips before drifting to the trees for the night.

A baby quail troops after his father

Then, in season, comes the cautious single-file parade of hatchlings up from the lower garden, next to the grape arbor. Under the cumquat, just under the comforting edge of a spreading juniper, a pair of quail had positioned their nest. The eggs have popped out tiny teetering fluff-balls, chicks who by are now are ready to move up into the larger world of the patio. The black-plumed caps topping adult heads jiggle like antennae as they lead their babies from the protected nursery, ultimately guiding them into the daunting vastness of the Catalina Foothills preserve. That will be their new home, where by instinct all quail belong. They carefully pass by the patio ramada, disappearing into the dense hedge haven of oleander bushes—exit route to the Great Outside.

That path alarms me, because the occasional transient bobcat also pads into that floral dimness. It's every animal's covered departure path from our walled garden. He doesn't come often—just checks in now and then for small live stuff. We will see our quail again later on, down on the road, busy crossing from one bushy hideout to another. The chicks lose their adorableness; they're entering their teens, bigger each day, skilled at ducking predators.

DAVE NEVINS PHOTOGRAPHY

The bobcat is no house kitty . . . even if he is on your patio

And so comes the bobcat. We sneak hushed to a window to observe his arrogant stalking stroll across the bricks. He is muscled, strong, catlike but not, and fine-looking. When my husband first saw him he said, "Come here! Look at that huge cat out there." But the bobbed tail identifies him as not a house cat. And he is big. He comes around looking, I think, for the odd grazing rabbit. Señor Rabbit finds cover under long leaves arching out from our tropical bird of paradise. The bobcat wanders on to the neighbors, dissatisfied with us.

They really do run on the roads out here...

But to me, the most surprising drop-in has been the roadrunner. The chaparral. Upon arrival, he peered carefully around a bush, then advanced slowly, placing one dainty foot in front of another, his spikey black crest leading his speckled body, trailing his long tail. Cocking his head, beady eyes checking side to side, he made his way to the water source. A quick hop, and up he went to the bottom lip around the fountain. A few dips and sips, and when I turned back—he was gone. His visits have been rare and wary.

Owls perform at night, hooting from their high watch on the iron gate. A flashlight illuminates their eyes ... they glow eerily. Annoyed, the owls silently flap off, insulted. Our cookout guests have been entertained. They head off into the desert nighttime, saguaros looming like guards. We go in to bed.

An owl surprises us one morning

As I pad my way to the cozy harbor of our pillowtop California king-size, its comforter pulled back to welcome my exhausted self (having company is work), I scan the floor for bitey bugs. You know—scorpions, spiders, that sort of wildlife. Even a centipede. Now, those are scary.

When we were about ten, my cousin Lee found and smacked an orange-legged black centipede at our grandmother's place in the Texas Hill Country, a locale perched on a bluff overlooking the Medina River, and home to such fanciful critters as armadillos and centipedes. It died, he boo-hooed over his cruelty (I was plenty glad it was dead, knowing its bite would be sincerely painful), put it in a cigar box, and buried it in the flinty Texas dirt with a sad little prayer.

I tried to see the spirit of centipede going up, but no joy.

Our Tucson home does not house centipedes or their ilk. Following valued advice, we hire pest control. You should too. You'll sleep better.

We love Tucson.

5 WILY COYOTE

The coyote is no dog—watch your pets!

We have, in our eco-protected residential area, a few handsome tawny coyotes who brazenly patrol our yards and driveways, occasionally catching a human's eye before fading into the pucker brush. They are fearless but happily non-confrontational. The coyote has a long history, formed over thousands of years as he ranged and multiplied across the lands.

I can just imagine the face of the archeologist who first assembled ancient fossil bones of *Canis latrans* and set a date of existence at somewhere between 150,000 and 400,000 years ago during the middle Pleistocene epoch. He must have realized he had the progenitor of our rascally coyote. Today's versatile and adaptable bush dog is the result of breeding and ranging over the western hemisphere, exuberantly creating more than nineteen varieties, including a mix from mating with his large cousin, the gray wolf. DNA has proved that. They're both from the *canis* family, and apparently friendly to each other.

But interestingly, they don't diddle with dogs. They eat dogs. They're much smarter than dogs, and will even create a tiring relay, taking turns with the chase, to outthink and outrun your pet. Not only that, they will temptingly lure that four-footed meat of yours, your would-be protector, with a coyote female in hot heat. Coyotes don't mate with dogs, but dogs cannot resist coyote pheromones. Anyway, that's how the group tricks our big ones. Coyotes hunt in packs, snapping up little yappy fluff balls. Keep small pets inside at day and night.

The word *coyote* comes from the Nahuatl Indian's name *coyotl*. He is also known, by the way, as the American jackal. He is crafty and tricky, portrayed as such by the western indigenous in their lore. The wolf has a far nobler reputation, somehow.

The city of Tucson, Arizona's ever-growing interloper of the plains, is currently home to about two hundred thousand coyotes (according to Arizona wildlife authorities) stretching out across the Sonoran Desert. Its reliable sunshine and warmth, so kind to aging joints, has called to seniors across the nation. The subsequent rise of accommodating buildings of home and hospital have crept relentlessly out across that desert. One must admit it—the city has encroached on wildlife; but they didn't leave. They were here first.

Of the desert menagerie, to humans, coyotes probably are the most obvious, slyly slinking around housing developments. Beware: he's not looking to merely riffle through your garbage. He's searching for meal-sized cats and dogs.

Few pets are equipped to match this hunger-driven ur dog. Our neighbors guard their fluffy lapdogs carefully. If one should sneak out, its fate could be written. *Canis domesticus* has a sad instinct to rush into the chase of prey ... to its doom—especially high-wired, frenzy-prone lapdogs, often favorites of seniors.

One evening a friend's smallest member of his pet trio, a sleek dachshund, naughtily whizzed out between his owner's legs, joining his larger buddies for a night's prebedtime widdle. Normally never off-leash, he saw a gleeful chance at liberty and grabbed it. His buddies were big German shepherd bruisers, well-fanged males probably capable of conquering almost any wildlife encounter— unless targeted by a clever hunting pack or puma.

Joyful, brave, naive, and foolish little dachsie.

He did not return.

At four in the morning, his anxious master was slowly searching the streets by car. Suddenly a coyote trotted across his headlights' beams. To our friend's horror, he saw his feckless pet's body-less head and chest gripped in the coyote's bloody fangs. He has not told this to his children.

Coyotes are surely there, eyes gleaming and focusing in the underbrush, looking and awaiting the careless move of an untended pet.

Thus the wily coyote survives and thrives. They roam nationwide. Years ago, in San Antonio, place of my birth, the local paper's police log reported a call from a woman in an upscale residential area. She, a warmhearted animal lover, was not having success feeding and bathing a homeless dog, and could the police come get him?

"He is just so uncooperative," she said emphatically.

The police snickered upon their arrival. "That's no dawg, lady. That there's a coyote." (He said "kai-yōt." More standard is "kai-yo-tee.")

Similarly, in rural Massachusetts, I was idly motoring home when suddenly a dog launched itself off an embankment, just missing its opportunity to cross safely, whanging into my right front wheel. It spun through the air and landed, twitching, roadside. I quickly stopped, everyone stopped. We all watched in terrible fascination as the handsome beast convulsed his last breath. No collar.

"You're going to have to call that in to the animal control, lady," huffed one oh-so-helpful onlooker.

"Naw, you don't neither," snorted another. "Hell, lady— that ain't no dawg ... thassa coyote," he declared authoritatively.

Then the woman from the car behind me—she of course had also gotten out—threw herself into it. "A coyote? Hey! Can I have it? My husband is a taxidermist."

The little group stared at her, murmuring and muttering. There was a bit of shuffling around, then a "Why not?" floated out. No reason I could see.

Nonplussed, I shrugged and said, "Be my guest."

Their eyes turned to her, to me, then to the furry corpse. I was relieved to be rid of any possibility of responsibility. I think it showed.

She snatched a large trash bag out of her trunk and with a bystander's help, quickly stuffed the corpse in, as though he might come to. He was thick-coated, handsome, muscular, and deep-chested. No wonder we figured him to be a pet.

The excitement over, the kerfuffle resolved, the dead animal rolling away in the taxidermist's wife's car, I too departed.

What an odd day.

From New England to Texas, from there to Arizona and beyond, the wily coyote prowls our neighborhoods for morsels. They eat our mice, rats, squirrels—and our pets.

Don't even think about trying to woo and tame one.

They are not our kind.

6 TUCSON STREETS

Once a young man asked his eighty-year-old grandfather, "Grandpa, how come you've lived so long? What's your secret?" He expected to hear something religious, dietary, or attitudinal—things Gramps usually preached about.

But Grandpa replied, "Oh, that's easy. I've never made any left turns."

Chew that one over.

From the East–West trade route Silk Road of the Far East, traveled by Marco Polo, and jumping ahead to El Camino Real, the old thoroughfare of our far West, humankind has traipsed around the globe for his myriad reasons, trampling out paths wherever he went.

For example, El Camino Real—the King of Spain's Highway—passed near Tucson. Those Spanish explorers were originally sent from the Old World to look for gold and claim more land for the expansionist monarchs. Missionary priests, too, went this way, possibly looking to reform those greedy explorers, certainly looking to convert the Indians to the One True God. (They left behind wonderful outpost missions in the Southwest, now striking historic relics.) Plenty of treasure for both groups, but no El Dorado here, no streets paved with gold.

But the grid of highways and byways that ended up overlying all this trooped-over Arizona territory has its own value, its own hint of gold, found in its clever layout and motorist accommodations. Of course, Tucson was lucky—it could start from scratch, on a huge flat palate.

Urban areas around the world all take a stab at managing traffic. The world did not foresee the marvelous car or truck, did it? Those have spawned great commerce, great growth—and a great mess. What came before was created to fit pedestrians, horses, and wagons. The advent of cars has required it to revamp every passage.

It has been difficult.

England has defined green belts to surround its cities, both to limit urban overgrowth and preserve nature's beauty. This involves one-way circuits around built-up areas to handle vehicle flow, ones where you must keep alert or as soon as you arrive at point B, your destination, you'll find yourself whizzing quickly back to point A, your startup. You have driven in, around, and out again before you know what's what. There you are again in the country-side moving rapidly in the wrong direction.

You panic.

How did that happen? Well, like this.

We were on our way to curtain time in Stratford-on-Avon for a performance of Shakespeare's *Merry Wives of Windsor*, tickets in hand and cutting the timing close. My husband, always eager to drive any nation's roadways, had been chuffing at me to get a move on. I didn't realize the tickets were *not* in hand but had to be picked up at the will-call window. The tickets would be given away if not collected a half hour before the show. So it was, that in missing discreet little in-town road markers, we whizzed a fast loop in and out of Stratford on its one-way system, as if we were on the end of a cracking whip. We were mentally wringing our hands and tearing our hair.

Me? I burst into helpless laughter as we foolishly disap-peared out of the urban into the farmlands, among Eng-land's famous hedgerows. Frustrated fury blew at me from my son and husband, which only made me laugh harder. It was the Miami Airport Syndrome, once identified when we looked though chain-link fencing across miles of runways while trying to get to Miami's distant terminals, takeoff time around the corner. It can happen any time you are frantically going away from where you want to be, lost, and can't find yourself.

How do you exit this bucolic route going to … where? Scotland? The signs were enigmatic to us foreigners. We were forced along by assertive Brits beeping those bleating horns as we rushed along, dazed, muddled, trying desperately to get it right. On the wrong side of the road, of course, because ancient habits die hard. Pre-autos, on horseback, the right hand was generally kept free to access your right-hand-wielded weapon. While trotting along perilous highwayman-plagued byways, you had to be ready for lurking danger. Change sides for a car? Why? Drive on the left. Later, Napoleon changed it, and the world followed. Not England. French 1, Brits 0.

England's antique streets, initially trodden down by Romans, then by wayfarers who morphed into horseback riders beating out the paths of the Middle Ages, have been paved. Those are the slow routes. New highways have superseded those byways, but the old ones are fun to poke around on, meandering along one-cart paths that might deliver you onto an overgrown World War II landing strip. Oh, it can happen.

The year was … well, back when. We were in England, adventuring on a sight-see through the Cotswold when our two-lane became a car-brushing one-track of pushy bushes and flitting birds. We curled uneasily around tree-shaded green hillsides, relieved to again come upon the better-traveled two-track. Unexpectedly the route widened into sunlight—and a giant span of concrete, edged by tall, unkempt weeds.

Ka-bing! The light bulb went off. "Hey—this is a runway!" we both exclaimed. We were on an erstwhile World War II runway absorbed into England's road system. The wartime Royal Air Force had many of these, mostly now defunct and overgrown, deep in the countryside.

As we poked along, by now nearing our destination Moreton-in-Marsh, we drove onto another of those huge runways—this one adapted to creative reuse as both a truck-driving training school at one end (lots of maneuvering room) *and a flight school of ultralights and microlights at the other.* It would never happen in the United States. When our airstrips close down, they become housing developments.

That's a bit of England's traffic tale. How about the French? French driving is almost calamitous.

There is an unwritten Parisian rule for maneuvering its avenues. "Never let another driver catch your eyes looking at him. If you do, you lose the contest of who goes first." Wild. That way the Citroën could dart out in front of you and know with certainty you would stop for him. I mean, what idiot would deliberately run into somebody? After all, he didn't see you, did he? They peer out of the corners of their eyes. Good peripheral vision is a must. Practice it.

How did France try to come to grips with vehicles and urban growth? When I was a teen, we lived in Paris. It was idyllic and romantic. But one could see that Paris was destined to become clogged with honking cars. The French love to honk. An avenue stopped up? A cacophony of claxons would arise in noisy pollution. Over and over, day after day. Know what? Honking got outlawed.

The Champs-Élysées

The system. The ground-level Périphérique, Paris's cobblestoned circumnavigating ring road, built when nobody could foresee what choking traffic problems were to come, finally outgrew its usefulness.

What to do? If one ring road was good, how about another? An elevated version was installed right over the original, adding another level of commuter clogs. And this, after decades before, the artistic brilliant French thought they had worked out how to handle all that. But they couldn't imagine the car.

You see, in the mid-1800s, the French, under new management—Napoleon III—simply threw up their gallic hands at Paris's shambles, and came to grips with their putrefying health-disaster poor neighborhoods. Several attempts to manage the city had been made in eras before, but nothing was permanent or successful. Now Napoleon III directed his prefect Georges-Eugene Haussmann to revamp the whole of the city. Out with crooked cobble-stoned alleys, down with leaning-over mansard houses, raze the stinking festering poor neighborhoods, and in with a star-shaped pattern of wide avenues. Add monuments and fountains, and of course eventual sidewalk cafés and elegant hotels. But it wasn't a cure, either.

In America, architect Pierre L'Enfant was hired on by our first president, George Washington. He planned a needed revamping of our capital, a marvelous visible witness to the new nation's power and ingenuity. However glorious and spectacular the plan, ultimately it didn't do a thing for DC's future motor traffic. Who could foresee? Just as ultimately Haussmann's glory didn't do much for a Paris of the future. Just took up generous tracts for monuments. Rather handsome, but useless for commuters. DC's traffic jams are things of nightmares.

But they cannot compete with the East—Mid, Far, or Near. Cairo is a torment, Delhi and Mumbai as well, and don't even think about Jakarta. Everything over there, really.

Mumbai (née Bombay)

South America's cosmopolitan Buenos Aires learned from those. This beautiful city has grand avenues lined with jacarandas, avenues wide enough to dedicate lanes for joggers, especially the morning ladies in warm-ups trotting out their stuff, ponytails bouncing. And large treed parks for dog groups and their sitters/walkers.

But best of all, our Tucson.

By 1900, a very rough-and-tumble Tucson could count all of 7,531 inhabitants. Imagine how that compared with New York, London, Rome, Madrid, Boston, Tokyo, Calcutta—the great metropolises of the world. In 1920, Tucson's population had soared to 20,292 ...and even in 1940, only 36,318; that's less than today's average East Coast suburb.

Without air conditioning and water pipelines, its sunny weather was not the people-magnet it is now.

With lots of land and few motor vehicles, Tucson's city fathers, visionaries who could see the coming vital role of cars, trucks, and buses, got a huge jump on the rest of the world. They built wide, straight streets—and to their ever-lasting credit, they designed every thoroughfare of any significant size with one or two ample left-turn lanes at every stoplight, with oncoming traffic stopped in every cycle to allow time for those with a green left arrow to make their otherwise chancy cross-traffic turns.

We may or may not live longer because of this, but every moment we spend in Tucson's traffic, compared to that elsewhere, is a walk in the park with birds singing and sage in bloom.

NB: Do not expect great road surfaces: any city worth the name has commercial traffic that beats streets to wretchedness, and Tucson is no escapee. It has its potholes and crumbles, but it works at repairs in a timely manner.

Gramps had it right. Get out and enjoy the city. It wants you to.

7 JAVELINA HAVEN

Pronounced "Havelina"

Off one of those clever left-turning spurs, our Tucson house sits in an area designated eco-friendly to desert plants and animals. Our street is an uncivilized, unimproved dirt road. Coyotes yelp in groups in the intense Southwest sunshine, sounding just like laughing boys as they scramble up the sides of the neighboring wash—at night too, and it's plenty disconcerting.

But not boys: danged coyotes. In the night, however, the bad-tempered, hideously fanged javelina (pronounced "havelina") also comes poking about, trailing its young, if it's that season. No denying they are incredibly cute in their warthog ugliness. I think the coyote leaves the javelina alone. Those amazing fangs are rippers.

This tusked beast likes to patrol *en famille*, sharp little hoofs trip-tripping across the road between washes, cruising warily between properties, sniffing for nice dead rats, foraging truffle-style with earth-moving snouts for tasty roots. We've seen hoofprints left from their rooting about in the dark of night. They're unbelievably tough, blissfully munching on thorny barrel cactus fruits.

They check trash bins for leftovers. My friend and neighbor once raised her garage door to a family of five. They froze in place while rummaging through her rubbish. They locked eyes. She glared a hands-on-hips "beat it."

DAVE NEVINS PHOTOGRAPHY

Javelinas poke around a backyard

Taken by surprise, they obliged. Mama javelina hurried them off down the hill and into the pucker brush.

She was lucky. They are known, when challenged, to offensively charge and gore with those impressive mouth tusks. You see, like famous Rupert the Rhinoceros, they're quite near-sighted. Probably they really aren't so fierce, but they can't see for their sniffing. Maybe they liked her scent. They have superior and discerning olfactory glands.

The nearsighted javelina—check those eyes

Those who know, like a Texas rancher friend, say they're as toothsome as the wild boar. You've seen those in European paintings of feasts, on a platter with the cliché apple in the mouth? In Mexico, local hunters of the countryside consider them a delicacy. Like pork. But know this: though variously called wild pig and skunk pig, they are not any type of pig. They are a variety of peccary, similarly hoofed but a different family. Way less friendly than Miss Piggy and friends. In the United States, javelinas are found only in our Southwest, but they proliferate throughout South America. The peccary is omnivorous, fanged, and mean. Similarities to pig exist, like that snout and close-set little eyes, but otherwise, not much else.

This saguaro-forested hillside neighborhood, sloping

upward from north Tucson's busy avenues, is a special place. When, years ago, entrepreneurial builders decided to create an architect-designed housing development, it was immediately designated by its homeowners' association as a de facto wildlife preserve. That is still in effect. And although its original houses may be way behind the times in modern accoutrements, they carry the cachet of history. And the nighttime view of the city is breathtaking. The wildlife, of course, including the near-sighted javelina, is unaware. They're low-movers patrolling close to the ground. (Occasionally we hear the bobcat on the roof—another story. Might he appreciate those distant city lights shimmering in the vast valley between far off mountain ridges?)

We watch for the javelinas' headlight-lit eyes as we slowly motor the road, being careful not to run into any trit-trotting family parade as we wend homeward.

Warning: Do not try to tame or feed them. Because of their unreliable natures, you could get into big trouble. Their near-sightedness could cause them alarming confusion. The news reported that a good-hearted animal lover in the Phoenix area is trying to recover from deep slashes to her legs, which her neighbors attribute to her feeding the ungrateful javelina, and which she does not deny.

Just enjoy the odd sighting and write home about that. Wisdom says it's not worth jeopardizing your tender flesh for a brag about a friendly ear scratch. You may want to cuddle a little one. Don't even think about it.

Javelinas don't understand friendly.

8 COCKROACHES HERE AND THERE

The Cucaracha, *or Cockroach—but Who Doesn't Know That?*

The American cockroach that lurks in our kitchens and burrows through trash bins is about an inch long and is just one of thirty varieties that plague us. There's also the disturbingly large version that, on longer legs, lumbers about throughout the South. Nearly mouse-size, they look possibly edible (if you're desperate enough). They are repulsive, repellant things.

And smart. There was one whose movement caught our eyes at the El Paso airport. He was scurrying intently across the terminal floor, skillfully avoiding large feet, aiming at the automatic door. Arriving at the exit, he paused to one side, seeming to wait for a human to activate his egress. We were fascinated. Someone came, the door opened, and he made his getaway. Clearly it was a process he'd used before.

A droll ditty exists about the cockroach, the popular toe-tapping Mexican "La Cucaracha" (origin unknown); according to one verse of the song, he's the critter that doesn't get around because he's out of marijuana. (For entertaining lyrics and history, search the internet for www. cecil@straightdope.com.)

The ubiquitous cockroach, brown insect of the 4,600-member order *Blattodea*, is a survivor of everything. He's known to have existed through life-threatening perils for 350 million years. It shifts its venue at will, living on dribs and drabs of anything. The cockroach has been known to lodge in furniture, even in a clock, and thereby change its residence with a cross-country move. They've been known to hitch a ride all the way from New York City (big center of infestations) to a new dwelling thousands of miles away. The unsuspecting homeowner dreamed of being rid of them, to have left them behind in his now abandoned dwelling. Silly twit. If the cockroach can live for years behind wallpaper, what's a clock to conquer? Its life, though threatened in today's world by countless poisons, continues undiminished.

It knows only to scour for food and propagate. Which it does abundantly, at night, mostly, furtively scuttling in dark places to nosh and poop, leaving behind its *E. coli* and/ or salmonella-tainted feces. Oh—and dysentery, among countless other contagions. Even dusty dried up cockroach poo can cause annoying issues, like asthma and allergies. It has no social bias. It burrows in slums on neglected garbage. It lives in kitchen cabinets of elegant homes in upscale neighborhoods.

Once years ago, at a League of Women Voters meeting in the most upscale town outside of Boston, I was asked to please look for coffee sugar in our leader's kitchen cabinet. Dutifully I went to the kitchen and opened a cabinet, thereby throwing light onto open boxes, marmalade jars, and cans—and onto an alarming, writhing blanket of small brown cockroaches, their antennae waving inside gaping cereal boxes.

I shuddered, closed the cabinet door, returned empty-handed to the living room, and avoided my hostess's inquiring eyes.

Faces turned toward me. I announced to the group that she was out of sugar.

Our cockroaches? In Álamos, Mexico, our home is free of them. Astounding, but there it is. If you are anti pesticide, I hang my head in quasi shame. But they are rife there, especially that big black tropical one—and it's them or us.

In drier Tucson, the moisture-seeking insect tries to access our house through drainpipes, an age-old sneak, probably since the advent of lead pipes in ancient Rome. We foil that by putting borax in drains, a desiccating and poisonous item for them. They collect and carry the powder away on their little hairy leg bristles where ultimately it dispatches them. That works.

Nothing like ruminating on the throne and having your eye catch the motion of antennae poking up through the shower drain, probing antennae leading the emergence of a coffee-brown, armor-plated, cringe-producing cockroach. They poke around, investigating possibilities, opportunities.

Next stop? Probably your toothbrush.
Get the borax.[1] It works.

---

1 There are valid arguments against borax, but I ignore them.

9 THE SNAKE EVENT

My tensed body on the *qui vive*, I panicked, shaking my husband's sleeping form.

"Eeeeeek!" I hissed at him. "There's a snake in the bathroom. He's essing himself across the bathmat."

My groggy mate raised his head in a "what now?" configuration.

It was midnight, and we were several months into nesting in our new-to-us Tucson house. It's a 1950s vintage structure, apparently with the odd tiny hole making a come-hither entry for a wee thirsty beastie prowling for water. We are, after all, in the crackling dry Sonoran Desert.

Daytime brings a pleasing flutter of thirsty birds to our patio fountain—besides the usual cloud of finches, we have several quail, sometimes a roadrunner, and a Cooper's hawk. *And* that stalking bobcat. The pool? Doves have drolly learned to use the Creepy Crawler pool float as a teetering perch to sip from. Saguaro cactuses loom around the house, magnificent in the daylight, other-worldly in the dark of night.

"What can we do? I don't want a snake in my bathroom!" I wailed and shuddered.

"Well, we can go back to sleep," growled my unenthusiastic mate, dropping his head back onto the pillow.

"Bloody hell, I'll not close my eyes with that thing slithering around who knows where." I glared at him. "Maybe it's poisonous." That got him up to look.

"It's gone," he said. I peered in after him. Uh-oh. He was right; it was gone. But *where* had it gone *to*?

It was a little thing, a small, stripey, pretty snake. It could hide anywhere.

I carefully, quietly, peeked and poked about. Aha. There it was! It had made its way behind the toilet. I didn't want to rile it—but I also did not wish to have it near my precious pink parts, nor my toes nor my rump. There were horror stories of pythons, pipes, and plumbing. I'd heard them all.

Burrowing back in the bed, I grabbed up my source of information, the dizzying data-driven iPhone, and typed into Google "How to get rid of a snake in the house?" To my amazement something like "Arizona Wildlife Protection, 24-hours" and a telephone number floated up in front of my eyes.

Expecting nothing, I called.

Whaddaya know? A groggy male voice answered. I explained my problem. He gave me another number.

This time a less groggy male answered and explained that, yes, he could remove the snake—for $110. Or, he said, we could just ignore it and it might go away. Probably would.

That was my husband's vote. Oh no, sweetie … not an option.

"Oh well, all right." Sweetie waffled, caved, and agreed that I should cater to my fears and hire the guy to come out. He can be such a mensch.

In no time at all, our expert appeared at the door, a tall, rangy, blue-jeaned fellow with piercing blue eyes and a shock of white hair. He ankled in, a remarkable Ted Danson doppelganger, bringing a simple empty gallon jug and long-handled pincers. A stethoscope hung around his neck. Our savior had arrived.

But where was snakey? Oops … no snake. Not behind the loo, not anywhere.

"You cannot take your eyes off the animal for an instant," he tut-tutted. "He could have gone anywhere at all." Looking around, he mused, "Baseboards are the most likely places." I noted floor-level gaps that small things could use for slithering up behind.

He knelt on the floor, folding himself up like a grasshopper, and, with flashlight in hand, scooched around on his knees. I envied his flexibility and said so.

"It's genetic," he replied, grinning.

Perseverance paid off. With a stethoscope he detected movement behind a baseboard. I got a pry bar from the tool supply, and off he pulled it. Little snakey turned out to be a harmless and useful mouse-eating king snake, but what did we clueless imports know? It quickly started to wriggle across the floor. Our herpetologist snapped it up with the pincers and coaxed it into the jug. It wasn't as easy as it sounds; Señor Snake was not cooperative, its wee head writhing vigorously away from the opening.

Once the scare was safely contained, our Ted Danson look-alike rocked back on his heels. He pointed at my book posters. I explained they were my Amazon-available opuses about my piloting, one as a Paul Theroux–type adventuring tourist in Australia, the other a fiction about a young woman falling in love with flying, stalked by a murderer.

He smiled and remarked that he had once taken flying lessons. He had hated giving it up—not enough time or money. "Yah no, I'd read that exploring one, but murder mysteries aren't my cup of tea." I figured. "He humanely saves snakes," tutted I to myself.

The quest done, the event quickly turned into a fun "Did you know?" and "Were you ever?" We had simply sprawled amiably out on the floor, leaning back on our elbows, feet stretched out, chuckling and marveling over small world connections. Right there in the quiet Arizona night under millions of stars, surrounded by desert varmints snoozing in their hidey holes—or not. We knew the dangerous fanged javelina liked a nighttime scrounge about. But at least one adventurous serpent was no longer a threat. Silly me, it never was. But how did I know?

We paid our fee gladly and saw the white hair off into the darkness, his figure lost against the saguaros as he climbed into his jeep.

How charming, how diverting, indeed how remarkable. The Tucson tapestry was weaving itself most agreeably.

10 TUCSON'S COZY CORNERS

Charm Is Where You Find It

They're tucked in about everywhere (ostensibly cockroach free; businesses seem to have a handle on that problem). If you poke around, you can find those niches of coziness and color, wafting alluring aromas and spreading *Gemütlich-keit*. Down a certain block and around a corner, out along an avenue away from the usual loop ... maybe in a park? Those little city pockets of delight that curry to your tastes of sight and palate. New York has them, San Antonio too, San Francisco—every city where humans thrive. Including Tucson.

Boston had its Cheers (oh, it was a real place, all right), San Antonio its Liberty Bar, Savannah had the old converted manse, Lizbeth's—all places where they knew your name and acted like it even if they didn't. Today there are coffee places where your mug hangs awaiting (one's in La Jolla). Or a beer mug? Tucson's Old Chicago on Campbell Avenue has your earned mug. Its bar and grill has fans who elbow each other for the best booths and barstools and folks who like to chat you up.

All smack of the hospitality you need, crave, when you're new—and still do when you've been around a bit.

But let's browse the marketplaces. The first I have in mind is the Mercado de San Agustin, a small off-downtown gathering place of locals and a few tourists, those few who happen upon it. It's away from Tucson's center at the foot of the landmark "A" Mountain. Inside, just beyond the Mercado's central patio, past artisan shops and boutiques, whiffs of coffee and toothsome Mexican pastry lure you in, inviting you to settle for a while. So you do.

The Mercado de San Agustin's central patio

"Buenos tardes, señores—que podemos ofrecer?" (What would you like, what can we offer you?)

The friendly cooks ply you with their good humor and delicacies. We grab a couple of yummy spiced cookies and settle in with coffee. There are chairs and tables edging the patio, and you peer into other venues of commerce.

"Oooh, honey, lookee there!"

My honey looks. With perked up interest. Through a plate-glass boutique window, we see a young teen trying on clothes, putting on a show. Finally she decides on a sleek satiny one that shows off her stuff in bas relief. All of it. Wow. We giggled, lips sugary with pastry bits.

"Hey, you voyeur," I mutter at my husband. He was peeking out of the sides of his eyes at the fanny-swishing teenybopper.

"That's a pretty dress," I say to the girl as she struts off. She acknowledges with a shrug. Hey—to her, I'm old, how would I know? A bored look flickers over her face.

St. Philips Plaza is home of the Saturday farmers' market where stands of honey, baked goods, and homegrown vegetables are the backdrop for cozy corners of good beer, good cheer, and amazing culinary creations. La Reforma and the Union Pub both have plenty of wide screens for sports watching if you're into that, and chatty bartenders. They seem to cater to a particularly friendly clientele. When Mexico was in the World Cup, Reforma opened early that Sunday morning with tequila bottles to the ready. Olé's and clapping, and new bar pals to be made.

Another agreeable refuge is in the Tohono Chul botanical gardens. A triumph of planning in itself, it is a spikey, spiny cactus-filled must-see for desert flora admirers, and home to a gourmet destination tea room besides.

Various city entrepreneurs have fashioned charming outdoor locales for both delectable adventure dishes and reliable comfort food. Tucked onto the edge of a huge acreage stroll of walkways, greenhouses, and sale tables, Tohono Chul sits amid giant shady mesquites. This café they picturesquely call a tea room, you do need to visit. Feast on an exotic salad or rich goopy enchilada. Then hit the gift shop. They sell items you just have to have, like jalapeño jelly—and maybe you'd like a string of red chili pepper lights?

The Tucson Botanical Garden holds its charming surprises, too. We strolled along carefully planned paths under grand old shade trees. We read identifying tags at the base of curious plantings, copious samples from Arizona's vast, enigmatic desert. That huge desert lies right out there, beyond this midtown oasis, even within the city limits. The helpful labels pull away the veil a bit from the things that manage to survive and thrive out there.

But there's more—these intriguing gardens are whimsically art filled. Check out the statues, review the walls, poke about in the specialty gardens, and finally, rounding the corner of a promising building, find … what's this? Why, food!

"If you enjoy our fare, we can cater an event for you," smiles the hostess. We had run across their creations at a special event, one that ultimately brought us to the gardens to seek out these chefs. Their small but colorful café pulls you in with promises of nectars, toasted sandwiches, fluffy salads—and desserts. All concepts of the moment, handmade, served with open-handed friendliness and hospitality. You'll want to go back.

Snuggle into Kingfisher Bar and Grill at happy hour for champagne and oysters—bartender Mike will know you well in no time. Get there early or you'll miss out. Mosey down the avenue to Speedway's Trident Grill near the UA for warmth and cheer from their bouncy youthful staff. And along the way is the Old Town's handsome Cushing Street Bar & Restaurant. Like warm and fuzzy? You'll love it.

And don't miss the historic Congress Hotel, the Southwest's once-upon-a-time lair for the infamous Dillinger gang. The Congress's gourmet Cup Cafe, a downtown gathering place, is so worth the frustrating parking effort. It has its own lot, but not on the nights when it's taken over by jazz fetes.

Set out exploring. You'll happen upon more cozy niches than we've had time to discover. There are super finds in this handsome, sprawling city.

Tucson wants you to be happy.

The plaza does Day of the Dead

▐▐ DOWNTOWN TIPS

Back in the day, a British bombshell crooned a winsome song. Petula Clark won our hearts with "Downtown" – she closed her eyes, tossed her head and gloriously belted out advice about when you're lonely, hitting the neon-lit sidewalks, going to the city's busy place, a vibrant place where you could meet someone, a place to surely forget troubles and cares.

Talk about centers of vibrant life, Tucson has got it. From its early days as a train stop, the station still lies alongside the tracks, a place downtown that fills your ears with romantic whoo woos of rumbling passing trains. Some even stop to let you board for parts afar. Creative reuse eventually spawned today's elegant Maynard's Market and Kitchen, home of outstanding bouillabaisse and clever treatment of quail. Landmark? Maynard's is across from the previously mentioned Congress Hotel's famous Cup.

Strolling along a block or two, you come to the esteemed chef Janos' Downtown Kitchen, a place of happy babble and good drinks – and his legendary culinary creations. Cheek to jowl seating strings out good times along the impressive mirrored bar, and you want to sit there if you can wriggle your way in. Our bartender Richard came up with a dandy fun drink for me, serrano infused gin with a slosh of Cointreau to soften its edges. You can feast there, too, or go over to a roomier table.

Next on our list of amazing is the Café Poca Cosa. Minimalist and elegant, the décor reflects its chef-owner, the elegant Susana Davila. She has been turning out her totally non-minimalist, indeed opulent, mouth-watering dishes for over thirty-five years. Her offerings change daily as her artistry moves her and are therefore written on a chalkboard. Poca Cosa has no handout menus. This restaurant, next door to a handy parking garage (make careful note of your level – don't get hilariously lost as we did) is a must destination for all visitors to Tucson, whether on business or pleasure. From Phoenix to Katmandu, everybody goes there.

Sra Susana Davila, A-1 chef for 35 years,
queen of all sauces, avocado to mole

*Mackenzie Dalton, a waitress at Gentle Bens Brewing
Company, poses with the restaruant T-shirt.*

Do you want to rub shoulders with the college crowd?
Not strictly downtown (and certainly not just for youth).
The gray hairs particularly know a good thing when they
find it—Gentle Ben's Brewing Company is a grand place
to lift your mood. Head up first avenue towards the UA,
and turn into University Ave and find Gentle Ben's on the
corner of Tyson. The edifice was built in 1908, the home
seriatim to a University president, fraternities, and dorms,
but as an eatery extant since 1971. It became a brewery
and restaurant of extraordinarily delicious pub food—all
aficionados of a great burger and/or the best reuben in the
USA. Don't forget a pint of outstanding ale, brewed on

the premises. You'll want to settle in here for a while. (The name? Came from a character on the TV show Grizzly Adams, who looked like the manager.)

There are others. Put on your adventure hat and go for it. All businesses in this book are locally owned; none are chains. Their policies, menus, and employment practices are not dictated in some far-away boardroom, but tailored to Tucson by people who love it here. Of course, chains can be good, too, but home is where the heart is.

12 DUST DEVILS, WHIRLWINDS, WILLY WILLIES

But Not "Willywaws"—Those Are Something Else

Dust devils are common in the desert plains

The worldwide plains of our continents are full of them, those mysterious winds of rising ropes of writhing dirt. Even oceans have them, where they're called water spouts. Skinniest of tornadoes, if you will, a whirlwind is a rotating tight spin of air sucking up loose things that then make them visible. Thermals, those rising columns of heat that top off with a cloud formation at condensation levels, can take that whirling dust up thousands of feet.

Once, flying north out of Mexico on approach to Phoenix at five thousand feet, we spotted one a mile or so off our wing, then a few others here and there in the hazy distance. I called the air traffic controller and expressed my surprise and awe. I could visualize his blasé shrug as he said, "First time out here, or what? We get those all the time."

The ones I remembered from childhood dotted the desert, reflected in mirages, and brought to mind cowboys and cattle and the song "Cool, Clear, Water." This was way different. I meekly responded with a "Roger."

Once there was a lively one on a taxiway at the Tucson airport, an oddity that appeared ahead of us, as thin as a pencil, erect as a telephone pole, moving along the route to our tie down. Was it dangerous? We stopped, mesmerized, and announced our dismay to Ground Control, then watched as it wandered off and dissipated.

"Yeah, we get those sometimes. They'll spoil your paint job," replied Ground.

From our hillside Tucson home in the Catalina foothills, selected for its fine view of Old Pueblo (Tucson's original name) and the wide Sun Corridor around and beyond it, now and then we spy a rise of dust, a fat puff stretching and spinning up into a vertical thread, coming off perhaps a downtown construction site. As the air mass moves it, a wind shift probably, the dust column is directed away from its source. It breaks up and falls away. Usually.

Sometimes they turn into those "devil not a man" things, showing us that the far west spirits are still there. Populate the plains as much as you will, you can't cover it up. The Tohono O'odham Indians, a large group abutting the peaceful Hopi, were here first; the Indian cultures influence life today. You find traces in names and beliefs. The dancing fertility god Kokopelli, the flute player, celebrated on tourist paraphernalia, is one. It was believed the hunchback tootled babies into being, and rain. You see, they say originally his flute was not a flute . . . Many of these agricultural peoples farmed in flash flood waters and mountain runoffs. Those thermals can rise up to bring storms, when there's enough moisture in the clouds.

It's said the flutter of a butterfly wing stirring the air can be the start of a storm, even of a whole weather system, if you follow the idea through. If that's so, can the passing of a car on a highway, its passage stirring dirt at roadside, be the start of a dust devil? Who's there to take notes? In the scorching breezes of the vast desert, I see no volunteers.

We do see twirling wind funnels spring aloft from tractor tracks as a telltale sign of agriculture. And then there are those rising from no geo-disturbance at all, nothing but heated air doing its dance, around and around. But the air is so dry that humidity is hovering around zero. Scant chance of a rain shower. Not from that plow, or that thermal.

If you look with eyes clear, then squint, sometimes you can see Kokopelli dancing with his flute through the lifting, expanding haze. They say the Tohono O'odham see him.

Maybe so do I.

13 FLORA, MOSTLY

The desert sage in full glory

The sun seeped in from behind the shutters. We flipped up louvers to greet the oncoming flood of light and jump-start the day with coffee, and take in the sight of nearby mountains, rising beyond faint silhouettes of mesquite and cactus.

I didn't expect more than the usual pink flush of dawn—but what was this? A fat foundation-planting shock greeted us with a cloud of color: masses of tiny blossoms streaming along each spikey branch. It burst upward like lavender fireworks.

It was desert sage. A memory of author Zane Grey and his *Riders of the Purple Sage* lifted out of my mind's haphazard shelving—there it was, at my window! But where are those cowboys?

I think round-ups, cowboys, and mustangs have been replaced by the jeep. But the sage endures, an important honey bee and hummingbird attraction. We have several fat bushes around our house that without any warning, they simply explode overnight into a purple wonder. We waft thanks through the cosmos to clever landscapers. Those clouds of misty purple, short-lived as they are, soften our landscape and the arid desert.

The saguaro dons its whimsical bonnets

They come into their own after the iconic saguaro has done donning and doffing its whimsical top bonnets of split red-tufted fruits, by-products of its crazy twenty-four-hour white blossom stage. The flower pollination process is rapidly taken care of by greedy nighttime feedings of long-nosed and long-tongued bats. Even the ends of those oddball structures' "arms" hold them out like bouquets, offering nectar for hummingbirds and seeds to cooing doves, juicy bits for javelinas, coyotes, finches, woodpeckers, and the like.

DAVE NEVINS PHOTOGRAPHY

(L) Birds perch on a barrel cactus while (R) a prickly pear cactus flaunts yellow camellia-like blooms.

Grab some binoculars and amuse yourself at these whimsical feeding stations.

At the same time, plump, deep-burgundy pears emerge, fruits of green prickly pears; they're the hip of a bright yellow camellia-like bloom. This cactus is called a tuna or *nopal* in Mexico and is also named a paddle cactus for its big, flappy leaf shape.

The fully bristled cholla cactus? That contorted shirt snagger whose needles locals swear leap to impale if you get too close, puts out a rich dark-red or purple rose of its own. Birds have been known to nest in the cholla. Somehow. Springtime brings a colorful cactus competition.

The dark pink rose of the cholla

Peeking out from between low scrubs you can glimpse mad flashes of bright red-orange, fat round clusters of hardy *tabuchin* or Mexican Bird of Paradise. Hugely decorative, they grow into large shrubs of poufy blooms, waving like pom-poms, and they're impossible to kill. They make a wonderful addition to any xeriscape garden.

Mexican Bird of Paradise blooms

Snug those up to sky-blue plumbago, another tough-flower act. They also sport flower clusters on the ends of branches. Plant them side by side, and you have something rather spectacular.

Plumbagos grow well in Tucson

Oleanders, too, proliferate. Once established, their water requirement is minimal. Our outdoors is bordered by a thick, high-growing hedge of the oleander. Underneath, in a friendly cave formed by their soft shadows, a community can take cover. Into the dimness lippity-lips the quivering rabbit, the head-dipping quail, and probably a slithery snake or two. But I don't think about that. The dense bushes importantly provide safety from the circling hawk, himself a striking passerby.

The oleander and the Mexican Bird of Paradise love Tucson. All along busy Campbell Avenue flourish both—the densest, highest, most flower-laden oleander and *tabuchin* bushes outside faraway Turkey or Mexico. Around town and around the corner, long-established thick trees of oleander efficiently screen a modest trailer park. Up the way, across the traffic, more arching branches wall off a bustling plaza of upscale stores and restaurants. These grand floral displays are all decades established; you'd do well to get started. Easy to install, easy to grow, and easy to keep going.

A floral carpet of verbena

Back on our patio, pushing out in a floral carpet from ground-level patio planters, dense purple desert verbena creeps out across the bricks. A most excellent ground cover, it grows copiously and thickly, a blanket-like home for the amusing *Sceloporus magister*, the desert spiny push-ups lizard. This small, startling reptile scurries to a halt, surveys the area, bobs menacingly up and down, then flees under the blossoms. Handy escapes for the whimsical macho lizard, the tough guy who does front-leg presses to assert himself. "Ok, little buddy," we say, "you're safe now."

Sceloporus magister, the desert spiny push-ups lizard

Thirsty hummingbirds dart and hover, braking to a mid-air stop and reversing for some flower sipping. Tall yucca spires have trumpet-like flowers that accommodate their long thin beaks. The blue agave (famous source of tequila) has also rocketed up its flowering spire, along with a gentle perfume to attract obliging pollen-spreaders. Lower garden aloes have also sent up batons of blossoms, easy drinks for both bee and bird. The yucca's spear-like leaves efficiently protect the plant, leather-stiff with dangerous blood-drawing points. No worries, big boys. We don't have enough of you to try our hand at tequila, anyway. Or the courage.

Not all our garden parts hail from the extreme desert. Champagne grapes droop in luscious clusters from their arbor, peaches are coloring up on their trees, and the kumquat has mouth-puckering golden fruits ready to be plucked. It all needs some water—we are, after all, a hydrosphere. But being climate-adapted here as in some other parts of the world, these orchard luxuries actually don't use much. The fruits we harvest often go to the neighboring schools. No waste. They're happy, we're happy. So are the birds. They find the grapes particularly toothsome.

Not all garden parts hail from the extreme desert

We who have been watching from the edges, loving it all, turn to each other and raise our coffees in salute, again sending silent thanks to those decades-ago anonymous landscapers who set up this dream, and applaud their wisdom in using the region's desert flora, habitat for Tucson's intriguing wildlife.

Maybe later we'll toast them with a bit of Don Julio Reposado. Only fitting.

*A butterfly feeds on nectar from a
Mexican Bird of Paradise*

14 FOOD, BEAUTIFUL FOOD—

I'M A FAN, AND I'M WEAK

TUCSON: BURGER TIME? Often my choice, but my oh my, what other delights are there. In Tucson, I can be easily lured off-track.

What it is about me, is this: (Besides, please Lord, deliver me from over-cooked vegetables.)

When I was little, sitting in my high chair with my parents at a restaurant on some cross-country move (restaurants were not usually part of my world), I was mournfully looking down at tired, steamed carrots (I'd of course already scarfed up the meatloaf) and drearily thinking of my promise to eat them. A sweet, well-meaning old lady beamed at me, leaned over, and said, "Oh, you sweet pretty thing, are those carrots what put the roses in your cheeks?"

I looked at her, glared back at my plate, and firmly declared, "NO. MEAT." I was taught not to speak to strangers, but this required action.

I reckon I haven't outgrown it.

Can such a bastion of flavorful Southwest cooking, a city

simmering with dishes of Mexican and American Indian influences, also be a harbor of destination hamburgers?

Oh yes ... for those whose palates recoil from the zesty chipotle, whose stomachs cringe at picante, Tucson has absolutely outstanding burgers.

Not the drab little flat thing McD's delivered from its golden arches so many years ago—but they did start the whole love affair, didn't they? How the hamburger has bloomed and morphed. Ever since bacon snuck its toothsome way onto the patty and vegetarians started packing edamame, black beans, avocados, and zippy spices into their own equations, we find outrageous explosions of palate-teasing pleasures. What hedonists we've become.

And Tucson has its share of tempting diet-spoilers, some listed here. One place that touts the patty in its name is Zinburger. There are two locations, waitressed by students, mostly female cuties switching about in short shorts. Kind of brings back how you used to be, before those years of burgers.

Angus or Kobe—your choice

There you find the succulent, unimaginably delicious Zin Burger. Its caramelized onions can be sautéed in heady zinfandel (Zinburger? Get it?) should you wish—so can optional mushrooms, as shown here. Homemade buns are fresh-baked from potato flour with a touch of honey. (Potato flour ... I remember the long-ago killer delicious glazed Spudnut.) The cheese, warmed Manchego, nicely fits itself onto the primo Angus or succulent Kobe beef patty—a type of Japanese Wagyu beef—all arranged on a cushion of delicately shredded lettuce. Even my lettuce-hater man likes it. The bed serves as an efficient sponge for the burger's savory juices. Soooo good.

Or travel down Campbell Avenue. The flashy neon of Old Chicago, that many-screened sports bar, home of famous thin-crust pizza, has beefy pleasures that go well beyond pizza. Look at that—my wondering eyes alight on an extraordinary beer burger, a conception topped with sauce made from Guinness and loaded with thin crispy onion rings. Well, everyone knows beer and burgers are a marriage made in heaven.

That's two for you, satisfaction way beyond the Wendy's, In-and-Out, and Burger King drive-thrus. But I'm not done.

For experiences headier yet, tuck yourself into the beautiful and upscale, historic Arizona Inn for its own special Inn Burger, enjoyed best in their Audubon room, off the sheltered patio where tweety birds patrol for table crumbs. Nobody makes them better. Want something less traditional? Maybe the smoked salmon platter with buttery multi-grain toast points, capers and chopped onions. Or the best chicken salad fleshed out with fresh berries. Or short ribs, or whatever you wish. Their chef does it all. A favorite delectable oddity … glazed, toasted brussels sprouts with thick goat cheese panna cotta. A bit singed around the edges, but drizzles of honey make it right. Not standard, not for everyone, but crispy delicious.

Down the way a mile or so there's the Trident Grill, an idea from the mind of a Navy captain and erstwhile Navy SEAL. Have the burger and come back again for the tenderest, sauciest Reuben. May be the best in Pima county. But tell them to dump the layer of coleslaw. Not really the thing, is it, when your mouth is expecting sauerkraut?

Or drive out Oracle to the Tohono Chul Park Tea Room, a place nestled on the edge of the Tohono Chul Botanical Gardens. Munch your succulent burger or salad under umbrellas in the midst of desert flora. Plan time for a walkabout. You'll love it all.

I realize there are those who are going to curl their lips at a burger and need to find another excellence, all available in Tucson. Need creativity and nouvelle? Try Feast on Speedway. One evening's sortie took me down a ruinous path to a table at Feast. Making our way to be seated, we passed an odd white, fluffy puff on a plate. Clouds of ... what? Our waiter grinned and said, "Cotton candy."

I had to have that. "Life is uncertain," goes the saying, "have dessert first." But it wasn't cloyingly dessert sweet— just lightly spun delectable. Clouds of sugar webs hid skewers of sautéed meaty tidbits. Then came rich short ribs and other entrées. The menu for these choices was delightfully opaque, the language foreign, idioms exotic. We needed the staff to lift the veil of mystery. Turns out Maestro Doug hunkers over his monthly changes and gleefully spins his own new culinary language to entertain and to impress his feastlings. Go for it!

Absinthe makes the heart grow fonder

We topped off the night with an elegant ritual absinthe, the fountain dripping nectar into little sugar-cubed glass sippers.

Chef Doug brought in a carnival machine to make the puffy clouds. He promises to bring it back.

Worth a big mention: Pastiche Modern Eatery, Firebirds Wood Fired Grill, Kingfisher Bar and Grill, and Wild Garlic Grill—all have chefs with extraordinary talent. And Chinese? The best, according to a good Chinese friend and superior cook is Years Asian Bistro and BBQ on Wetmore. Asian fusion: a smart thing.

For steaks, we tend to sidle into the long-established south side's Silver Saddle, a complicated find off I-10 on an access road at the Benson highway. It was there before the Interstate, and potential patrons have to deal with how to get there. People figure it out. Like many outstanding steak places, they have a visible smoky mesquite grill to rouse your taste buds. In the other direction, Fleming's is a step up in ambiance, worth the trip north for their noisy happy hour bar menu. You may actually find honest prime cuts there, not the faux USDA Choice cuts passed off as the real thing in many steak houses.

Some are crazy about Mexican food, that which goes beyond chips and salsa. Hankering for the tongue-tease of jalapeño and signature ambrosial cilantro, they troupe up in phalanxes of fandom. Lines at Mi Nidito on the south side wait patiently, testifying to its excellence; the Guadalajara (good live mariachi music) as well as Rosa's also fulfill lusts for guacamole, enchiladas, and mole. Of course, there are plenty more, the influence of the region being so imbedded. Mexican fusion? You can't get better than the Baja Café, hiding at the back of a strip mall off Campbell on the north side (there's another location at Ina and Thorneydale for you northwest Tucsonians). Crowds gather; Sunday mornings are the most popular. The wait is worth it.

Go Mexican—chili today and hot tamales

Restaurants and their servers have come a long way since I had a job in the Northeast as a reviewer. For example, once, when we were served burned potatoes, the waitress waved us off with a "Yeah, they're coming through like that a lot these days." Huh? And at another place, we ordered red wine with our pasta marinara. The waitress brought a rosé, a resolutely pale-pink product. When confronted, she shrugged and said, "Well, so? That's kinda red, idn't it?" That stole our mojo. With that, any rejoinder from us was short-stopped.

And another, when insisting on cash, no credit card, and we asked what if we couldn't scrape up the cash, snorted, "Curiosity killed the cat," and turned her back on us. We got it together, but you can bet no tip.

Back in the day, rudeness was rampant. No longer so,

with the power of ratings. Probably never was in Tucson. They understand good business, and folks here are eager for you to have a nice night out.

Provecho! Bon appétit! Move over, New York. Tie on that bib and have at it. Get going, patrol down the avenues for a place to wrap yourself around. My personal default treat? A mouth-watering cheeseburger, dripping with juicy flavor, maybe with a hot side of ketchup-dipping crispy fries. Ahhhh.

15   OYSTERS, OYSTERS EVERYWHERE

Or the Rule of OysteR

Some of us are oyster addicts, yearning hopelessly for the gray flaccid treasure lolling moistly, inertly in its rough little casing, the shell lined with a subtle shining nacre, poor cousin to the shimmering abalone's. But the succulent meat of the oyster way outshines the abalone, that rubbery delicacy of the Caribbean. Abalone fritters? Only if you're desperate. The oyster comes in toothsome stews, elegant spinach creations labelled Rockefeller, and the mouth-watering naked pleasure of nestling oysters on crushed ice plates, cocktail sauce at the ready. But those stupid oyster crackers: their raison d'être totally mysterious.

My personal affliction took hold when I was two-and-a-half and my Army Air Corps mission-flying daddy returned to Ohio from New Orleans with his crew, bearing a gallon jar full of freshly shucked oysters. They swept me up onto the kitchen counter to perch beside the jar, grinningly offering a slippery morsel. They knew full well that of course I would be revolted by their sliminess and looked forward to my wails of protest. Silly men.

I remember how big the men were, and how they crowded the little kitchen. While they debriefed among themselves about their DC-3 junket to the South, I dipped in to help myself to more. I greedily slurped down about a quarter of the jar before they noticed. In horror, they saw what I had done, and rapidly plopped me onto the floor. My mother giggled and patted my little blonde head.

It was the beginning of a lifelong, worldwide search for more perfect oysters, a reprise of that pre–World War II moment in that kitchen.

On Australia's Gold Coast, there were oyster shooters, wallowing in sake and wasabi. Then there were New Zealand South Island's bluff oysters, a gustatory destination unto themselves. Truly, it's said New Zealand grows the best of the best.

But it's a tad out of the way, no?

As is South Africa, home of the biggest oysters we've ever seen. *Huge.* We were on a motoring tour of South

Africa, a nation full of marvelous beasts and vistas. This stop wasn't on the list of must-dos, but a coastal town? That called to us. It was on our track.

Knysna, rife with marinas, fishing boats, and a plentitude of bars and restaurants, pulled us in. Turned out it offered the most enormous and delicious oysters we'd ever seen. We stuffed ourselves and waddled out nearly delirious with our discovery. Years later, in Tucson's Scordato's Pizzeria, we met a man who lived just uphill from Knysna. He knew about these oysters. Together we had a glassy-eyed moment, dreaming memories of far away. You never know who you'll meet, where.

Now, we settle for Northern Hemisphere troves. And there are plenty. Maybe not so huge, but surely as flavorful.

Our favorite haunts for the fattest oyster lie all around the continent. Our first find was the Old Ebbitt Grill in Washington, DC, play place of news folk and congressmen in the shadow of the capital building. The Ebbitt usually flaunts a menu of six imports.

Then we have Texas with their Gulf oysters, and of course, New Orleans, where it all began.

We've been lucky with our finds. Just down the road from Álamos, our charming Mexican town, there's a source on the Sea of Cortez. Shrimp as big as your fist and gloriously large oysters. We do indulge, from time to time.

But in Tucson's dry Southwest, far from the oceans, how could we sate ourselves? Aha! They import, of course, from everywhere. To reliably satisfy cravings in Tucson, we aim at Kingfisher Bar and Grill's imports, or Casa Valencia that trucks them up from Mexico. Equally good is Sullivan's Steakhouse. All have decent oysters, but sadly the rule of *R* is written in stone in North America. I have a story ...

Once, overnighting in Fayetteville, North Carolina, en route to a Christmas in Texas, we were directed to Fayetteville's popular 316 Oyster Bar. We were so enthralled with the succulent oysters spread before us, we had two dozen each. Ooooff. So when flying past there again a few months later, we stopped to indulge ourselves again at the 316. Mouths watering, we ordered a dozen each. We anticipated the same excellence we'd found before. But no. What were placed before us were wee marble-sized niblets, not the eye-popping wonders of six months before. What was the problem? We summoned the waitress.

"Gee, 'at's the way they's comin' th'u these days," she said.

Baffled and annoyed, we asked to see the manager.

"Hey, we made a special trip to have your great oysters," we whined to him. "What's this miserable offering, those pea-sized things?"

"Oh, ah'm so sorreh—we kin give yuh an extruh dozen to make up fuh that. But yuh see, this idn't thuh raht season for oystuhs and we are not puhmitted to get them from thuh public bids. So we buy them from private bids, jes' tuh have em, since folks expect us offuh oystahs. You know that rule? In months with AHR, oystahs ahr in season. This heah is June, an' the oystah idn't grown big yet. No 'ahr' in June."

After downing the sad offering, and muttering between us about this horrid development, the light went on. *Bids* was southern for *beds*! Oyster beds. And we had totally forgotten the Rule of OysteR.

Those tiny things show up in Tucson as well. We try to control our lust till we enter the *R* months. We have a wait. But wait! West Coast oysters don't abide by that rule! Better beds, better weather, better business? Never mind— just roll 'em out! Tucson provides.

16 MONSOON

Monsoon over Tucson

Monsoon, a hot weather phenomenon of stupendous South-west thunderstorms, is a time of trembling dogs scurrying to hide in closets, or maybe just cowering for comfort by your knees. They hate that ear-pounding, floor-vibrating din. The family once had a peach of a friendly golden retriever who tried to escape the racket by hiding under cars. RIP, dear doggie Pandora. Once a tow truck had to be called to raise the car to get her back home.

The phone had rung; it was the police.

"Mother," called out her son, "have you seen Pandora? Can't find her anywhere." We were visiting her home in Concord, Massachusetts; there had been an early morning thunderstorm. Pandora was infamous for disappearing at cannon booms on Patriot's Day—and during thunderstorms.

"Missus Cabot? We got your dog down here, I think. She's under a car and won't come out. The driver is kinda upset. We've tried everything, but she's not movin'."

A discussion ensued, and mother agreed to pay for a tow truck with a lift.

In Tucson, it's the season of rushing waters scouring dusty arroyos and runoff waters that leap from banks and cover low bits of roadways. Terrifying in their violence, sometimes those outflows swallow cars, and you'd best not be in one. It's a time of hope and excitement for this parched place, a time when electricity charges the atmosphere with zippy negative ions. Those ions stimulate cilia in your ears and nose, making you feel perky and happy. Did you know that?

When I was little and dark clouds rolled in, cool downdrafts brushed our cheeks as we youngsters ran jumping for joy in the first fat sprinkles, sticking out our tongues to catch a drop. We joyfully whooped and jumped, bounding around like baby lambs till our mothers scooped us up and dragged us inside. Ah, childhood. Now we stay in and watch the show through the windows.

Monsoons have their own season? Yes, Tucson has five seasons, not four. Fall, winter, spring, summer—and monsoon. Five. I have that on authority.

Apps are made for your cell phone whose notifications are whimsical rumbles, warnings if any storm action is in the offing. Also, the app will notify you of nearby lightning, or tell you that you need to scramble for high ground if you're in a flood zone. We are reminded that floods can happen way downstream from the deluge; around dry Tucson, water rolls off the mountains.

NOAA also patches in texts of alarm for high wind gusts and hail, naming places to avoid. You can get maps of lightning strikes, cloud cover, and distance from the nearest display.

Dark storm clouds pose imminent threat of flooding

"Quick! Grab a chair, Maudie!" Best to seek solid cover when close by, not just a ramada. You settle yourself on the patio to watch the light show, cloud to ground bolts splitting the black sky. And you stay on the *qui vive* to hightail it indoors when the forecast proves right.

No garage? Well blanket up your car, do your best

to avoid hail damage. Nature's showtime can extract a tiresome price.

The deluge comes. If you're lucky, the barrage can be wild and wonderfully overwhelming. Puddles turn to pools, pool surfaces dance with the downpour, snakes slither out of flooded holes and seek high ground, usually draping themselves over your sun-heated driveway. Watch out.

The afternoon's oven-hot air that drove birds to find shade under patio chairs, that nice spa temp for the cold-blooded snake, has now climbed aloft and cooled at condensation levels. Clouds have bloomed and become towering rain factories, firing off decibels of radar returns from their busy cores. You can hear it happening. Aircraft, beware.

Cloud buildups rise over mountains near Tucson

Earlier, you watched as buildups rose. Little white puffs began to peek suggestively over distant ridges. Then

you saw them pooch out and billow up. They continued
rising, reaching high over peaks. They spilled over, crept
toward you, escalating to fanciful cloud towers. That
dazzling white suddenly morphed to threatening gray, slate
floors for castellating turrets, the odd thick veil of rainfall
sweeping out below. Were they coming your way?

Looks like it, doesn't it? That app could have told you.
The air is split by a ripping bolt, and the dog heads for the
closet.

Grab a chair and enjoy the show. From inside, through
a window. When the performance is over, it's not. Now
comes the finale. The most stunning, explosive sunsets
you'll ever experience are right here in Tucson. Corals trail
across the sky, flamingo pinks pouf at clouds' edges and
purple streaks above them. Shimmering golds and silver
trim the mountain peaks, and in a few moments it fades
and winks out.

It's all over till the next one.

17 TUCSON AND HEALTH CARE

You're sick? Oh no.

No worries.

Be reassured that Tucson is humming with excellent medical care. Each urban quadrant has a competent, well-received hospital. Truth be told, that's why we, and so many others, find it comfortable and reassuring to settle onto this hot plateau of cactus and chilis—besides titillated palates and stunning vistas, that is. It's just that we humans are occasionally wobbly, and we have to feel we have quality care to fall back on.

After all, Tucson is renowned for its medical care. The University Medical Center UA took the world stage in 1985 when Dr. Jack Copeland inserted the first early version of the Jarvik 7 artificial and temporary heart. But hopefully you won't need that.

First, let me tell you about the hospital ERs. You know, those places where you scurry for help when you're sincerely frightened about a possible removal by the grim reaper. He's always there, waiting patiently with his scythe, threatening your earthly existence.

TLC at TMC

Sometimes it's a terrifying battle to keep him at bay. We're rarely ready to leave. We're like Hamlet, unwilling "to shuffle off this mortal coil." I mean, what's beyond that veil? Hell, heaven, or high water? Or nothing?

We take up arms against our demise, and Tucson's modern medicine is there to help. Few of us are like my adored mother-in-law, who, at a seasoned 102 years old, had tired of her battle against the constant mundaneness of her life as it had become. She quietly asked her son, my husband, "Can't you give me something so I can die? Everyone I ever knew is gone." She spoke sadly. "The last of my Kentucky Derby group is gone. They're all dead, every single one of them," she murmured, fingering her handkerchief.

Her favorite friends had gathered yearly at her house to sip Mint Juleps, sing "My Old Kentucky Home," make little bets, and wildly cheer on their picks. Slowly, one by one, they withered and died, slipping off the slippery slope, leaving her behind. "I've lived too long!" she would announce mournfully. We didn't think so, as fond as we were of her. She was our touchstone.

We were at lunch. Shocked, my husband reared back and said, "Mother, no! You're healthy. I cannot murder you! They'd put me in jail! If you want to die, then stop eating—like your neighbor did on Martha's Vineyard." RIP, dear Drew, intelligent and fun good neighbor, who—having stroked away the ability to speak and move properly—called it quits. With many decades behind him, he'd reached a good age for it anyway.

She mused a moment, shook her head, and said, "No, I can't do that." She looked at him fondly and stirred her ice cream. "The food's too good."

And so it is. We fight the fight, life will have its way. She was a dear heart, and we're glad she kept eating. She brightened our lives till she was almost 107, saying her farewells in the caring arms of a cherished granddaughter. I miss her.

So what happens when your doc is on holiday? Well, oops.

Not to worry—the on-call staff of doctors and nurses are hop-to-it ready for you. Quite the best of the best.

Your doctor's practice is, of course, closed when your emergency hits. It's one of Murphy's laws. The answering service contacts the physician on call; she sends you to the ER.

But maybe you don't want to hang out in that ER waiting room, a snuffling place teeming with disease, enduring those often twiddlingly looooong antsy minutes (hours?) that can feed your anxiety. Most likely you are *not* at death's door, and the triage staff will put you at the end of the line.

Take a number.

But if you are indeed critical, they'll roll you right in. Otherwise, do try an urgent care, the down-the-street doc-in-a-box. They're even listed in Yelp, with reviews and ratings. That's your first chance to sidestep that scythe. You go there for a bout of flu, a nasty knee scrape, a painful sprain. That staff is also at the ready, usually supplied with basic machines and labs to examine you thoroughly, and personnel qualified to peer at your bloods and prescribe something for your comfort. They can put you on your way again to wellness.

But if you are too sick after all, and need a more qualified MD? They'll boot you to that ER.

I've had the opportunity to test out both. The staff and employees in all places were kind and courteous, the treatments I received prompt and efficacious.

I prefer the smaller urgent care places—hospital patient waiting rooms are too much like giant petri dishes. That said, it's true that most check-in desks will require and give you a face mask for coughs. But after one professional described my pneumonia/bronchitis as CAP (Community-Acquired Pneumonia), I prefer to stay away from known-to-be ailing crowds.

But that's just me. And sometimes you don't get that choice. Take your own mask with you. Drug stores have them.

Carry a little pocket-sized bottle of hand sanitizer. And use it, hmm?

18 TUCSON GUARDIAN ANGEL

When being raised by my solidly conservative parents, people I can confidently declare members of Tom Brokaw's greatest generation, they advised me never to discuss politics or religion in polite society. Simply not done, was the rule.

Polite society. What's that? If one were to believe one's lying eyes, there is none left to be found. Rights activists decry Christianity, protesters loudly chant against Islam, the social media is infested with Russian hackers bound to stir America's pot, and it's a pot that simmers a stew of discontent, which people avidly read and believe. It's a free-for-all out there. Uncontrolled kids feel free to sass and punch a teacher. Respect has become perverted. Others pick up a gun and run amok. Television flouts violence: it's a culture of "monkey see, monkey do."

And the spirit of humanity goes begging.

So that opens the door to one of my favorite subjects, the guardian angel. You think you don't have one? Think again.

Unless you're so ba-a-a-d you think only evil, you surely have one. Don't believe it? Doesn't matter if you believe it or not. Hovering behind the scenes, waiting to step in where he or she can, you have one. Often disasters are smacked head on, events for learning. Your angel doesn't interfere with those, much as you might wish it.

Think of it this way. You are equipped with a guidance system from the cosmos, a.k.a. your inner voice, your intuition. Some avow prods from the Holy Spirit. You know, those scalp-prickling moments when your inner alarm says, "Blrrrt, blrrrt, don't get in that elevator!"—and if you're smart, you don't. Pity the ninny who wasn't paying attention, wasn't tuned in, or shook off the warning with a frowning, self-admonished, "Don't be silly," and maybe ends up robbed, raped, or dead.

Not all help is that dramatic. And I contend we folk are meant to be angels to each other. I will share a recent encounter of my own. Right there in a Safeway parking lot. You'll swear I'm crazy, but here goes.

The Tucson afternoon was smoking hot, and we had shopped. Now to shift groceries from cart to car. In the process, I slipped and fell. The tarmac was so hot the surface literally sizzled my feet. I had slipped off my sandals to get up more easily—big mistake.

In going to the deck, my husband had been a handy grab; I clawed him down with me. We both roundly thwacked our sacroiliacs; somehow hips and shins got into the mix. Voicing dreadful pain, groaning on the hot oily blacktop, I figured this was it. Yep—finally my old seasoned bones had broken, and I would need to plaster up and be put in traction. After a long life of damage-free tree falls, ski spills, and stair stumbles, woe, woe, woe, the luck had surely run out. Arthritic points of contact were screaming at me. I hollered back.

My unladylike yowl had drawn a small crowd: "Are you OK, lady?"

"*No,*" I sputtered, wailing.

Cell phones came out of pockets to dial 911.

Then something most extraordinary happened. A stranger appeared and stood over me. Quickly he crouched down and placed one hand on my shoulder, taking my head in his other, and brought his face close to mine. As if by silent mandate, I placed my hand behind his head. His eyes locked on to mine; his penetrating gaze filled my consciousness, along with an odd warmth.

He commanded, "Let the peace flow in." Again he said, "Let peace come in."

And so I did, and it did. Peace, the peace that "passeth all understanding," swept through me, and pain vanished into nothing. How could this be? Remarkably, I was all right.

Someone's arms came behind me to lock and lift me up,

but I exclaimed, "No! No! I'm too heavy!" Never mind—I was absolutely ignored. Behind my back, those unseen arms grabbed under my armpits, in front of me my husband's hands took mine, and in a rush, like a weightless feather, I was whished upright and standing.

I looked about to find my helper: he was nowhere. *Nowhere.*

I wasn't left unmarked by our fall. I say *our* because as surely as my coccyx thumped the tarmac, so did my poor husband's when I pulled him down with me. But he didn't hit as hard. Later I peered at fading black bruises and pondered the man who was there and wasn't.

And I reflect on that healing peace.

My guardian angel stepped in for me.

I know what I know.

You see, I have met my guardian angel. Years ago on a search for spirituality—it's said man is three things: body, mind, and soul (spirit)—I found a haven of meditative prayer, a place of comfort and solace in the hills of central Massachusetts. St. Joseph's Benedictine Abbey, home of prayerful monks whose whole cause is to simply pray for humankind, offered a chance for me to find resolution to my seeking.

The abbey is a draw for many in its area, providing religious services and counselling as well as delicious products for sale, good things emanating from huge bubbling vats in its commercial kitchens. It also houses a fine brewery, following the path of its brother abbeys in Europe, a brewery that turns out a hearty stout good enough to put a wide smile on the most particular.

It was in their books and jams store that I met my guru,

Father Theophane, a very tall, long-limbed, sandaled monk on sales duty. I had come to the abbey, traveling across the countryside on recommendations from a friend, to look for a book on meditation.

"Well, lookee here," said I to myself, salivating. "Here is a scrumptious display!" So at the same time I was seriously on my spiritual search, I was so pathetically distracted. What was that? "The devil is in the details," goes the saying. Sigh.

I was buying a jar or two of my favorite rhubarb-strawberry jam. ("Lead us not into temptation," says the Lord's Prayer. But I am weak.) The monk pointed me to a book called *Finding Grace at the Center*, sold it to me, and wrapped it to go. Then he looked at me with hollow El Greco eyes, out from under his monk's robe hood. It was a kindly face.

"You should read this. But I can teach you to meditate."

We had weekly consultations, where he both taught me how to focus and clear my mind, a complex process, and how to write my meditations and reflect on them.

One day he said, as I challenged him on the subject of guardian angels, that I needed to go home and meditate upon mine.

"I have a guardian angel?" I queried.

"Of course," he replied. "Clear your mind of everything, concentrate on nothing, then think of your angel. He's God's guidance system."

I did as instructed, until finally my mind's eye held nothing but a cloud of pure white. I thought then of my guardian angel. A strange, lumpy shape appeared slowly through the mist, a curious shape that meant nothing to me. A voice in my mind, loud and clear, said, "You don't recognize me, do you?"

I said I did not.

Suddenly a sense of enormous love overwhelmed me. The voice said, "I am your guardian angel, and I look like this from all the blows I have taken for you."

I reached toward it, but it receded and faded away.

When later I recounted my experience to my teacher, I asked him, "Does everyone have a guardian angel?"

He thought for a moment, then looked sorrowfully at me from under his cowl. He said, "I believe it's possible that some are so inherently evil, so against goodness, that they do not allow goodness in."

"Oh," said I. "Then how about demons?"

He looked intensely at me and said, "I do not discuss that. There is nothing more that the devil wants than for us to open the door to him by mentioning his name. So I do not. And neither should you."

I remembered my mother saying, "Do not speak of the devil; do not give him house."

Because of that, when years later Auschwitz was a tour stop, I declined. The reek of evil pervaded every atom of that place. Not for me to "give it house."

My inner voice, my guardian angel? Said not to. I know when to listen. You probably do too.

19   LET'S GO TO THE RACES

The bugler sounds the "call to post"

In the early 1940s, a restless time of war for our nation, desert Tucson remained a rather small western community. It was a place of ranches, dude and otherwise, a place under a dome of healing clean air, where Eastern doctors sent tuberculosis patients to recuperate. A place where a private school for girls and boys sprang up, ranch style, where rich people from all over the country could send their offspring along with their very own horses to board, far away from and protected from the temptations of civilization. Never mind that they could also bring their riding skills up to speed.

The Wild West had changed. Its frightening winds of lawlessness had been calmed; gun-slinging psychopaths had been conquered (in 1934, the downtown Congress Hotel had seen the capture of the infamous Dillinger Gang). Cattle rustling was under control—and indeed a successful rancher, a Mr. Jelks, had turned his interests to the horse as well as herds of cattle. With an eye to the bottom line, as well as humoring his own penchant for the horse race, he dedicated a chunk of his wide-spreading lands to an enterprise he called Rillito, a fenced-in oval track named after the nearby river. He equipped it with stables at one end and a tiered grandstand on the side, where he and other racing aficionados could gather and watch riders spur their horses into frenzies of competition. Turned out the community loved it. It was a huge success, and in ensuing years it took its place in the National Historic Register.

The clubhouse has live entertainment while you wait

And it truly is historic, a huge part of the world's horse history. Rillito Park was the birthplace of today's quarter horse racing, its straightaway chute system the standard now for all such races.

Though the photo finish comes last, it is not least—the photo finish was invented at Tucson's Rillito Park race track. What would the horse racing world do without that?

The six-week race meet starts early in February, when cowhands and riders joyfully invade. We regular folks haul on our cowboy boots and Stetsons, and the colorful west comes alive again. This is the fun time of Tucson—if you never do anything else, you should clamber up the steps, make your way to the betting booths, and listen for the red-jacketed, top-hatted bugler to sound the Call to Post. The tune he plays? "Boots and Saddles." Yep—a relic from the days when buglers awakened the troops, it was the first call of the day. It became a tradition: in 1841 our United States Army snagged it from the Brits who use it for parade call. Now today you even hear it trumpeted out at the Kentucky Derby. Interestingly, it was derived from the French *boute-selle*, "saddle up!"

Life is short, fill it with as much fun as you can. Yes, the gem show has become a staple—but can it bring the thrill of thundering hoofs and a chance to win?

Anyway it's only for a few days.

So if you must, go get your bauble—and then let's be off to the races!

CONCLUSION

A view overlooking Tucson on the drive up Mount Lemmon

Our Tucson time of discovery is not at an end and surely never will be, but perhaps a moment has arrived to reflect upon our southwest adventure. What has it brought us, how will it continue? We still find delight in the city's niches and corners of art and cuisine; we treasure the new friends we've found while scrambling to make sense of our lifes' new chapters. We've cruised into a contentment and happiness we never imagined we'd find, and look forward to more of that every day. By day a beautiful breakfast at home whipped up by our right hand gal, or a fanciful burrito ordered and eaten down the street at the tex-mex haute cookin' Baja Café? Or do we potter down the avenues to incredibly fresh berries and agave syrup-dripping hot cakes at Tohono Chul? Could the Arizona Inn's smoked salmon platter or a tender omelet framed by avocado, or crispy polenta be our day's gustatory start-up? Jump-start coffee at home of course; the second, a hearty and rich steaming cup at our elbow, will be next.

And thus fortified for the day, we'll sortie down into the town's talavera collections for colorful saucers, or maybe not. This might be the day to drive up Mount Lemmon for the tremendous views; or will we dig into the amazing Desert Museum? We don't get enough of that one, with its splendid dioramas and wildlife exhibits. Did I mention that before? It's a world-class answer-filled presentation for all the questions you might have about the area, as well as data you might not have imagined. If the road so lures us, maybe we'll poke about one of any of the handsome state parks festooned with amusing and stunning cacti—and fat little sagebrush.

So Tucson, the beautiful city spread across the United States southwest plains, still charms us. Tonight we'll bend our elbows with friends and wrap ourselves in their smiles and hospitality. Because no matter how splendid your surroundings, you need the warmth of your tribe to keep you going.

The adventure continues. Welcome to Tucson!